In the Spotlight

Malala Yousafzai

by Kaitlyn Duling

Bullfrog Books

Ideas for Parents and Teachers

Bullfrog Books let children practice reading informational text at the earliest reading levels. Repetition, familiar words, and photo labels support early readers.

Before Reading

- Discuss the cover photo. What does it tell them?

- Look at the picture glossary together. Read and discuss the words.

Read the Book

- "Walk" through the book and look at the photos. Let the child ask questions. Point out the photo labels.

- Read the book to the child, or have him or her read independently.

After Reading

- Prompt the child to think more. Ask: What did you know about Malala Yousafzai before reading this book? What more would you like to learn about her after reading it?

Bullfrog Books are published by Jump!
5357 Penn Avenue South
Minneapolis, MN 55419
www.jumplibrary.com

Library of Congress Cataloging-in-Publication Data

Names: Duling, Kaitlyn, author.
Title: Malala Yousafzai / by Kaitlyn Duling.
Description: Minneapolis, MN : Jump!, Inc., 2018.
Series: In the spotlight
"Bullfrog Books." | Includes index.
Identifiers: LCCN 2018004326 (print)
LCCN 2018003201 (ebook)
ISBN 9781641280488 (ebook)
ISBN 9781641280464 (hardcover : alk. paper)
ISBN 9781641280471 (pbk.)
Subjects: LCSH: Yousafzai, Malala, 1997
Juvenile literature. Girls—Education—Pakistan
Juvenile literature. Pakistan—Social conditions
Juvenile literature. Girls—Violence against Pakistan
Juvenile literature. Women social reformers Pakistan
Biography—Juvenile literature.
Taliban—Juvenile literature.
Classification: LCC LC2330 (print)
LCC LC2330 .D85 2019 (ebook)
DDC 371.822095491—dc23
LC record available at https://lccn.loc.gov/2018004326

Editor: Jenna Trnka
Designer: Molly Ballanger

Photo Credits: Karwai Tang/Getty, cover; Monica Schipper/Getty, 1; AFP Contributor/Getty, 3; Dave J Hogan/Getty, 4; TRINACRIA PHOTO/Shutterstock, 5; Imagenation Abu Dhabi/Parkes+Macdonald/Participant Media/Kobal/REX/Shutterstock, 6–7; Abdul Majeed/Getty, 8; Handout/Getty, 9, 23tl; Aamir Qureshi/Getty, 10, 22r; Wael Hamzeh / Epa/REX/Shutterstock, 10–11; DAVID HARTLEY/REX/Shutterstock, 12–13; IBL/REX/Shutterstock, 14–15; WPA Pool/Getty, 16–17, 23bl; Patrick Hertzog/Getty, 18, 23tr; Odd Andersen/Getty, 19, 23br; Wael Hamzeh / Epa/REX/Shutterstock, 20–21; onair/Shutterstock, 22l; JStone/Shutterstock, 24.

Printed in the United States of America at Corporate Graphics in North Mankato, Minnesota.

Table of Contents

Malala

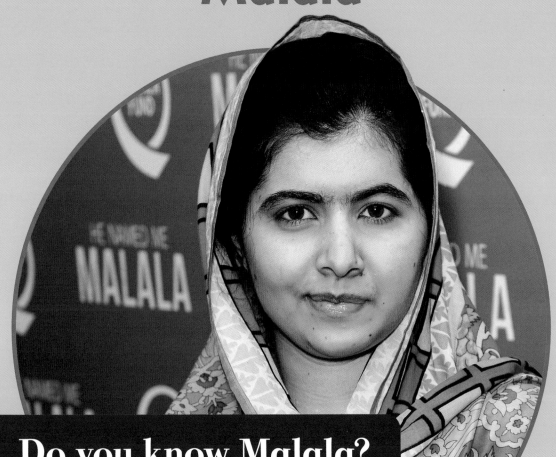

Do you know Malala?

She is brave!

Pakistan

She is from Pakistan.

She grew up there.

Malala reads.

She writes.

She wants all girls to learn.

She is from Swat Valley.

Girls could not go to school.

She spoke out.

family ·····▶

People tried to hurt her.

She lived.

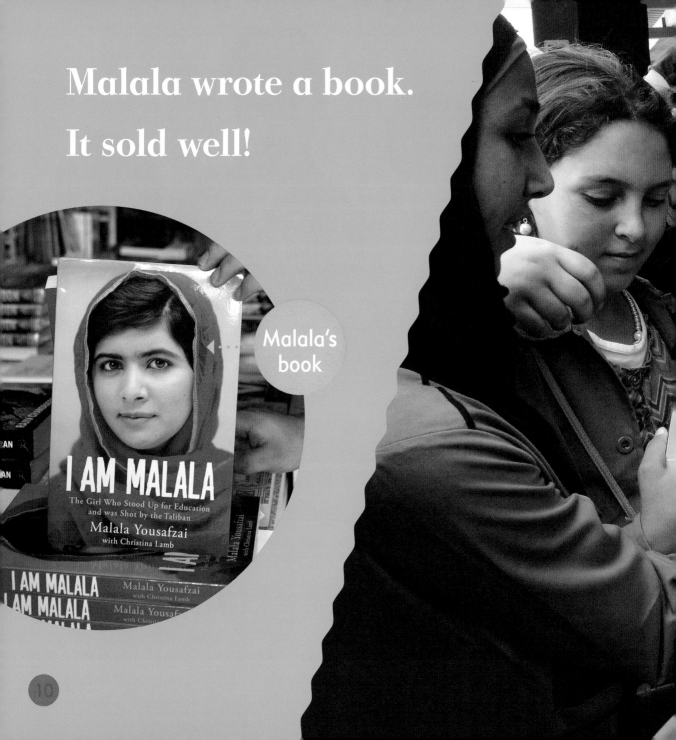

Malala wrote a book.
It sold well!

I AM MALALA
The Girl Who Stood Up for Education
and was Shot by the Taliban
Malala Yousafzai
with Christina Lamb

Malala's book

She went back to school.

She gives talks.

Malala writes.

She learns.

Queen
Elizabeth II

She is famous.

Many people
know about her.

She is young.

But she inspires people of all ages.

MALALA YOUSAFZAI

2013 WINNER OF THE SAKHAROV PRIZE FOR FREEDOM OF THOUGHT

LAURÉATE 2013 DU PRIX SAKHAROV POUR LA LIBERTÉ DE L'ESPRIT

PREISTRÄGERIN DES SACHAROW-PREISES 2013 FÜR GEISTIGE FREIHEIT

WWW.EUROPARL.EUROPA.EU/SAKHAROV

She won the Nobel Peace Prize!

Nobel Peace Prize

Den Norske Nobelkomíte
har overensstemmende med
reglene i det av
ALFRED NOBEL
den 27. november 1895
opprettede testamente tildelt
Malala Yousafzai
Nobels Fredspris
for 2014

Oslo, 10. desember 2014

Malala works hard for girls.

Thank you, Malala!

Key Events

July 12, 1997:
Malala Yousafzai is born in Mingora, Pakistan.

October 9, 2012:
Malala is shot by a Taliban gunman as she rides home on the school bus.

July 12, 2015:
Malala opens a school for female Syrian refugees.

December 19, 2011:
Malala wins Pakistan's first National Youth Peace Prize.

October 8, 2013:
Malala's book *I Am Malala* is released.

April 10, 2017:
Malala is chosen as the youngest-ever United Nations Messenger of Peace.

Picture Glossary

brave
Having courage and willing to face danger, difficulty, or pain.

inspires
Influences and encourages people to achieve or do something.

famous
Very well-known to many people.

Nobel Peace Prize
A prize awarded to a person or organization that makes outstanding contributions in peace.

23

book 10

brave 4

girls 7, 8, 21

hurt 9

inspires 18

Nobel Peace Prize 19

Pakistan 5

reads 7

school 8, 13

Swat Valley 8

talks 14

writes 7, 14

To Learn More

Learning more is as easy as 1, 2, 3.

1) Go to www.factsurfer.com

2) Enter "MalalaYousafzai" into the search box.

3) Click the "Surf" button to see a list of websites.

With factsurfer.com, finding more information is just a click away.